ME IN 4 SEASONS

A Journal for Your Journey of Change

D1280274

JOHN
HAYNES III

MOTIVATION FOR YOUR JOURNEY

Too many of my folks are suffering in silence! Day in and day out, you journey along needing help, but opting for silence! Stop being afraid of being judged! There's nothing new under the sun....not even your problems, predicaments, or hurt! Ask for help, run for help, crawl for help, cry out for help! I need you to survive!

Self-destruction is indeed an option...just not for you or me!

Life is much like writing and editing, in that, you live it, then go back and review it from time to time to see if you have done it right and what can be done better. *Then, you go correct the errors! Live prolifically!*

I caution you – do not assume that maturity simply comes with getting older! It is necessary that we grow on purpose; and, that we pursue the ability to respond to adversity with wisdom and without collapse in order to leap to greatness and reach the fullest of our potential!

MY GRATITUDE

God, for planting a seed in me – long before I arrived – and placing people, places, and circumstances in my life to water the dreams and let some of them come to pass. And, thank you for sparing my life just long enough to discover my purpose and help some people./My wifey, Gwen, for helping me stay in school; for saying yes to marriage and trying your hardest and giving your best to make it to forever; for the "black coffee" (courageous conversation) and the push to birth all that is inside of me; for taking care of our home; for our son; and for your beauty, intelligence, and your potential./ Super Miles, for being the best son and for bringing greater purpose to my life./Mom, for the sacrifices, your faith, your labor, your love, prayers, your example of work and service, and your pure will to survive./Dad, for passing along the gift to relate to all people and be a counselor, and the lessons you taught me even in your death./Stepfather, for a life pleasingly outside my expectations; I am the wiser for it./My brother, Garrett, for helping me learn how to care for someone other than myself. Eleven years of age difference is not enough to separate us./Rob, being the closest thing to a brother that a cousin could be; for the protection and wisdom; and for the real talk – no matter what./Big Rob, for teaching me that a man that doesn't want to be beat can never lose, and that, one day, it'll be my turn to burn./ Darryl, Marcus, and Phil, for being cousin/brothers and being your own men./Corey, for being somewhat responsible for me meeting Gwen; for your example and your mission to just help people; and for your friendship and "familyship"./Haynes family, for never forgetting about me and loving me unconditionally./Kwame Alexander, for letting me help you so that you could help me; you are universal inspiration and motivation./Lisa Anderson, for the constant exchange, partnership, support, and leaps of faith that make others leap./Sherron Washington, for collaborating on the formation and visual presentation of the brand and the hard questions that help make for great products./Jen O'Brien, for your "glitter" inspiration, your consistent manner of making dreams come true, and for being a cheerleader./My Facebook supporters who "like" nearly everything I speak into the universe: Laura Lane-Unsworth, the Klaus twins, Milo Hartley, Duane Samuda, Mike Moles, Kimberly Lyons-Butler, Swani Jessell, Lucille Bonita Davis, TaRhonda Harrison, Angie Hackey, Melissa Bracey, and Jacob Blauer./All coaching clients and those who have entrusted me with their weaknesses, vulnerabilities and successes – knowing that I would say something or offer some insight to make circumstances better or at least help develop a plan to address the issues fearlessly./Every leader with whom I have ever worked and served, you all serve as my daily "how-to" manual and my mentors!/My failures and enemies, I appreciate you more than I can express; and, I constantly keep you close and get to know you intimately – without keeping you in front of me./Alpha Phi Alpha Fraternity, Inc., I represent you in all that I do.

RULES OF ENGAGEMENT

Welcome to your journal for your journey! I appreciate you for tuning in and being available to your change, full potential, purpose, further development, and evolution – that which I am in pursuit of daily.

The words that you will read and hopefully ingest over the next 52 weeks are intended to make you think, feel, study, interpret, and take action towards a better you. And while you're working on the betterment of your mental, spiritual, and physical welfare, you will simultaneously have the opportunity to impact, influence, and perhaps enhance the lives of those around you.

As you read each post, know that the passages, motivations, and inspirations have been developed from a wealth of experiences (personal and those of others), tribulations, lessons learned, wisdom gained, failures, successes, days of fear, moments of triumph, and in pursuit of purpose. But more importantly, these thoughts on paper are meant to live – and they cannot live on and serve their mission if you do not put them into action.

With that, should you choose to journey on, the following is intended as guidance as you integrate this journal into your life:

• Invest in your desire for change and to make a difference in your own life.

• The journal is broken down into 52 passages, which correspond to 52 weeks in the year. There are four chapters, which are representative of the four seasons (but, are actually themes of the passages). Finally, there are 13 passages in each of the seasons. At the end of each season, as well as at the end of the journal, you can summarize the wisdom you gained and the change in yourself and others.

• Read one entry per week (purely suggestive). The week allows you to focus on the passage and your personal mission as to the meaning of the words. And, the time frame gives you the opportunity to take action on the words.

• Intend on meditating on the passages throughout the week – it may take you a day or two in the week to determine just what the words and thoughts are trying to say to you.

• As you process the words, use your entire life – mental, spiritual, and physical – as reference points for understanding the passages; the notions are meant to address the total person.

• There is no right or wrong interpretation to the passages. Through this journal, document what you think and feel.

• If the words don't mean something to you in the week that you encounter them, keep living, and the lesson and some attachment to the words may arrive.

• Know that what the passages mean at the moment you encounter them may change, evolve, and expand – as you continue to live – once exposed to that particular passage; and that's okay.

• Make it your personal mission to gift the passages to others. The words that may have some significance for you can be life-saving to others or shed light on their situations and circumstances that others are coping with as well.

• When good things happen, duplicate the success and be consistent until you own the positive changes that develop.

• Have fun further developing the best you!

winter

Change Is upon Me

It is time to dig up the old, till the soil (which is you), and soften your heart – making it ready to receive revelation and change. This is the exact time to engage your initiative, resilience, perseverance, and commit to the promise that better days are ahead of you and that YOU will be the instrument through this journey that will be used to facilitate YOUR transformation. It is time to get to work!

WEEK **ONE**

Every morning that you realize you have been afforded another breath is an opportunity to breathe life into people and your purpose! We are naturally designed to give life...do what is natural and just watch what will be born and renewed!

FRAMING QUESTIONS
Spark introspection, self-conversation, interpersonal conversation, and intentional action by answering these questions:

What do these words mean to me? How do they apply to my life?

_____

_____

_____

_____

What themes and takeaways do I have from reading this message?

_____

_____

_____

_____

What action will I take today/this week to apply and live these words?

_____

_____

_____

_____

What have I actually done in the past seven days to live these words?

_____

_____

_____

_____

What change have I seen in myself as a result of bringing these words to life over the last seven days?

_____

_____

_____

How do I plan to be different now that I have meditated on and ingested these words?

_____

_____

_____

Whose life did I impact and influence over the last seven days as I brought these words to life?

_____

_____

_____

*Who, specifically, could benefit from these words? I sent this message to _____ (name(s)) on _____ (date).

WEEK **TWO**

Listen! Stop leaving the believing up to someone else! The most important person who needs to see your hope and faith is YOU! And, others will then be inspired by your example!

FRAMING QUESTIONS
Spark introspection, self-conversation, interpersonal conversation, and intentional action by answering these questions:

What do these words mean to me? How do they apply to my life?

_____

_____

_____

_____

What themes and takeaways do I have from reading this message?

_____

_____

_____

_____

What action will I take today/this week to apply and live these words?

_____

_____

_____

_____

What have I actually done in the past seven days to live these words?

_____

_____

_____

_____

What change have I seen in myself as a result of bringing these words to life over the last seven days?

_____

_____

_____

_____

How do I plan to be different now that I have meditated on and ingested these words?

_____

_____

_____

_____

Whose life did I impact and influence over the last seven days as I brought these words to life?

_____

_____

_____

_____

*Who, specifically, could benefit from these words? I sent this message to _____ (name(s)) on _____ (date).

WEEK **THREE**

That we fumble, falter and fail is beautifully human. Our foibles let us know that perfection is not the path or the purpose. Excellence is indeed the direction of the journey!

FRAMING QUESTIONS
Spark introspection, self-conversation, interpersonal conversation, and intentional action by answering these questions:

What do these words mean to me? How do they apply to my life?

_____

_____

_____

_____

What themes and takeaways do I have from reading this message?

_____

_____

_____

_____

What action will I take today/this week to apply and live these words?

_____

_____

_____

_____

What have I actually done in the past seven days to live these words?

_____

_____

_____

_____

What change have I seen in myself as a result of bringing these words to life over the last seven days?

_____

_____

_____

_____

How do I plan to be different now that I have meditated on and ingested these words?

_____

_____

_____

_____

Whose life did I impact and influence over the last seven days as I brought these words to life?

_____

_____

_____

_____

*Who, specifically, could benefit from these words? I sent this message to _____ (name(s)) on _____ (date).

WEEK **FOUR**

Please afford me the vision and the courage to circumvent myself before I short-circuit myself! I will not be my own worst enemy! Now, you say it!

FRAMING QUESTIONS
Spark introspection, self-conversation, interpersonal conversation, and intentional action by answering these questions:

What do these words mean to me? How do they apply to my life?

_____

_____

_____

_____

What themes and takeaways do I have from reading this message?

_____

_____

_____

_____

What action will I take today/this week to apply and live these words?

_____

_____

_____

_____

What have I actually done in the past seven days to live these words?

_____

_____

_____

_____

What change have I seen in myself as a result of bringing these words to life over the last seven days?

_____

_____

_____

_____

How do I plan to be different now that I have meditated on and ingested these words?

_____

_____

_____

_____

Whose life did I impact and influence over the last seven days as I brought these words to life?

_____

_____

_____

_____

*Who, specifically, could benefit from these words? I sent this message to _____ (name(s)) on _____ (date).

WEEK **FIVE**

Those of you who are wishing so desperately for the future certainly cannot be putting everything you possibly can into today, the only thing that is certain and that you can do something about!

FRAMING QUESTIONS
Spark introspection, self-conversation, interpersonal conversation, and intentional action by answering these questions:

What do these words mean to me? How do they apply to my life?

_____

_____

_____

_____

What themes and takeaways do I have from reading this message?

_____

_____

_____

_____

What action will I take today/this week to apply and live these words?

_____

_____

_____

_____

What have I actually done in the past seven days to live these words?

_____

_____

_____

_____

What change have I seen in myself as a result of bringing these words to life over the last seven days?

_____

_____

_____

_____

How do I plan to be different now that I have meditated on and ingested these words?

_____

_____

_____

_____

Whose life did I impact and influence over the last seven days as I brought these words to life?

_____

_____

_____

_____

*Who, specifically, could benefit from these words? I sent this message to _____ (name(s)) on _____ (date).

WEEK **SIX**

Would you act any differently if you knew that you had a starring role in a miracle? Well... new day = miracle! Your move!

FRAMING QUESTIONS
Spark introspection, self-conversation, interpersonal conversation, and intentional action by answering these questions:

What do these words mean to me? How do they apply to my life?

_____

_____

_____

_____

What themes and takeaways do I have from reading this message?

_____

_____

_____

_____

What action will I take today/this week to apply and live these words?

_____

_____

_____

_____

What have I actually done in the past seven days to live these words?

_____

_____

_____

_____

What change have I seen in myself as a result of bringing these words to life over the last seven days?

_____

_____

_____

_____

How do I plan to be different now that I have meditated on and ingested these words?

_____

_____

_____

_____

Whose life did I impact and influence over the last seven days as I brought these words to life?

_____

_____

_____

_____

*Who, specifically, could benefit from these words? I sent this message to _____ (name(s)) on _____ (date).

WEEK **SEVEN**

For the source and solution to your recurring problems, check your recurring thoughts!

FRAMING QUESTIONS
Spark introspection, self-conversation, interpersonal conversation, and intentional action by answering these questions:

What do these words mean to me? How do they apply to my life?

_____

_____

_____

_____

What themes and takeaways do I have from reading this message?

_____

_____

_____

_____

What action will I take today/this week to apply and live these words?

_____

_____

_____

_____

What have I actually done in the past seven days to live these words?

_____

_____

_____

_____

What change have I seen in myself as a result of bringing these words to life over the last seven days?

_____

_____

_____

_____

How do I plan to be different now that I have meditated on and ingested these words?

_____

_____

_____

_____

Whose life did I impact and influence over the last seven days as I brought these words to life?

_____

_____

_____

_____

*Who, specifically, could benefit from these words? I sent this message to _____ (name(s)) on _____ (date).

WEEK **EIGHT**

Rise and shine...it is not only your command
for the morning, but it is your direction
for living!

FRAMING QUESTIONS

Spark introspection, self-conversation, interpersonal conversation,
and intentional action by answering these questions:

What do these words mean to me? How do they apply to my life?

_____

_____

_____

_____

What themes and takeaways do I have from reading this message?

_____

_____

_____

_____

What action will I take today/this week to apply and live these words?

_____

_____

_____

_____

What have I actually done in the past seven days to live these words?

_____

_____

_____

_____

What change have I seen in myself as a result of bringing these words to life over the last seven days?

_____

_____

_____

_____

How do I plan to be different now that I have meditated on and ingested these words?

_____

_____

_____

_____

Whose life did I impact and influence over the last seven days as I brought these words to life?

_____

_____

_____

_____

*Who, specifically, could benefit from these words? I sent this message to _____ (name(s)) on _____ (date).

WEEK **NINE**

I understand that the cycle of negativity, self-dislike, self-destruction, or lovelessness has traveled its way to you. But you do not have to ride that cycle any further! Love and faith are all-terrain and all-weather vehicles in which you can journey for the duration!

FRAMING QUESTIONS
Spark introspection, self-conversation, interpersonal conversation, and intentional action by answering these questions:

What do these words mean to me? How do they apply to my life?

_____

_____

_____

_____

What themes and takeaways do I have from reading this message?

_____

_____

_____

_____

What action will I take today/this week to apply and live these words?

_____

_____

_____

_____

What have I actually done in the past seven days to live these words?

_____

_____

_____

_____

What change have I seen in myself as a result of bringing these words to life over the last seven days?

_____

_____

_____

_____

How do I plan to be different now that I have meditated on and ingested these words?

_____

_____

_____

_____

Whose life did I impact and influence over the last seven days as I brought these words to life?

_____

_____

_____

_____

*Who, specifically, could benefit from these words? I sent this message to _____ (name(s)) on _____ (date).

WEEK TEN

I hear you! You do not feel like being introspective. But you do not have to be afraid of what and who you see in the mirror! You can change! I see the potential and the beautiful possibility of evolution in you! Uncover your eyes and vow to love what you see!

FRAMING QUESTIONS

Spark introspection, self-conversation, interpersonal conversation, and intentional action by answering these questions:

What do these words mean to me? How do they apply to my life?

_____

_____

_____

_____

What themes and takeaways do I have from reading this message?

_____

_____

_____

_____

What action will I take today/this week to apply and live these words?

_____

_____

_____

_____

What have I actually done in the past seven days to live these words?

_____

_____

_____

_____

What change have I seen in myself as a result of bringing these words to life over the last seven days?

_____

_____

_____

_____

How do I plan to be different now that I have meditated on and ingested these words?

_____

_____

_____

_____

Whose life did I impact and influence over the last seven days as I brought these words to life?

_____

_____

_____

_____

*Who, specifically, could benefit from these words? I sent this message to _____ (name(s)) on _____ (date).

WEEK **ELEVEN**

Stop running away and you can find yourself right where you take a stand!

FRAMING QUESTIONS
Spark introspection, self-conversation, interpersonal conversation, and intentional action by answering these questions:

What do these words mean to me? How do they apply to my life?

_____

_____

_____

_____

What themes and takeaways do I have from reading this message?

_____

_____

_____

_____

What action will I take today/this week to apply and live these words?

_____

_____

_____

_____

What have I actually done in the past seven days to live these words?

_____

_____

_____

_____

What change have I seen in myself as a result of bringing these words to life over the last seven days?

_____

_____

_____

_____

How do I plan to be different now that I have meditated on and ingested these words?

_____

_____

_____

_____

Whose life did I impact and influence over the last seven days as I brought these words to life?

_____

_____

_____

_____

*Who, specifically, could benefit from these words? I sent this message to _____ (name(s)) on _____ (date).

WEEK **TWELVE**

The life of promise you were afforded yesterday is not promised to you tomorrow! Get to living today – in this very second!

FRAMING QUESTIONS
Spark introspection, self-conversation, interpersonal conversation, and intentional action by answering these questions:

What do these words mean to me? How do they apply to my life?

_____

_____

_____

_____

What themes and takeaways do I have from reading this message?

_____

_____

_____

_____

What action will I take today/this week to apply and live these words?

_____

_____

_____

_____

What have I actually done in the past seven days to live these words?

_____

_____

_____

_____

What change have I seen in myself as a result of bringing these words to life over the last seven days?

_____

_____

_____

_____

How do I plan to be different now that I have meditated on and ingested these words?

_____

_____

_____

_____

Whose life did I impact and influence over the last seven days as I brought these words to life?

_____

_____

_____

_____

*Who, specifically, could benefit from these words? I sent this message to _____ (name(s)) on _____ (date).

WEEK **THIRTEEN**

Labor gets hard! It is even life-threatening! But it is gratefully, gracefully, and powerfully life-giving! And because there must be birth and rebirth, we must continue to push!

FRAMING QUESTIONS

Spark introspection, self-conversation, interpersonal conversation, and intentional action by answering these questions:

What do these words mean to me? How do they apply to my life?

_____

_____

_____

_____

What themes and takeaways do I have from reading this message?

_____

_____

_____

_____

What action will I take today/this week to apply and live these words?

_____

_____

_____

_____

What have I actually done in the past seven days to live these words?

_____

_____

_____

_____

What change have I seen in myself as a result of bringing these words to life over the last seven days?

_____

_____

_____

How do I plan to be different now that I have meditated on and ingested these words?

_____

_____

_____

Whose life did I impact and influence over the last seven days as I brought these words to life?

_____

_____

_____

_____

*Who, specifically, could benefit from these words? I sent this message to _____ (name(s)) on _____ (date).

spring

I Am a Farmer

You accept change and desire to be obedient to the opportunity before you; and, you want to plant and grow purpose and awesomeness within you. So, from this moment on, you are also a farmer and your mission is to continue to plant greatness in you – daily and weekly – which will create the change that will have you come face-to-face with your purpose!

WEEK **FOURTEEN**

Proactively plant seeds for the trees and flowers you want to see grow! Your seeds are love, faith, courage, relationship, time, second chances, and patience! And, we are to water our seeds daily with the same!

FRAMING QUESTIONS

Spark introspection, self-conversation, interpersonal conversation, and intentional action by answering these questions:

What do these words mean to me? How do they apply to my life?

_____

_____

_____

_____

What themes and takeaways do I have from reading this message?

_____

_____

_____

_____

What action will I take today/this week to apply and live these words?

_____

_____

_____

_____

What have I actually done in the past seven days to live these words?

_____

_____

_____

_____

What change have I seen in myself as a result of bringing these words to life over the last seven days?

_____

_____

_____

_____

How do I plan to be different now that I have meditated on and ingested these words?

_____

_____

_____

_____

Whose life did I impact and influence over the last seven days as I brought these words to life?

_____

_____

_____

_____

*Who, specifically, could benefit from these words? I sent this message to _____ (name(s)) on _____ (date).

WEEK **FIFTEEN**

Two people who are not afraid to talk to one another can go anywhere in the universe...just by way of conversation!

FRAMING QUESTIONS
Spark introspection, self-conversation, interpersonal conversation, and intentional action by answering these questions:

What do these words mean to me? How do they apply to my life?

_____

_____

_____

_____

What themes and takeaways do I have from reading this message?

_____

_____

_____

_____

What action will I take today/this week to apply and live these words?

_____

_____

_____

_____

What have I actually done in the past seven days to live these words?

_____

_____

_____

_____

What change have I seen in myself as a result of bringing these words to life over the last seven days?

_____

_____

_____

_____

How do I plan to be different now that I have meditated on and ingested these words?

_____

_____

_____

_____

Whose life did I impact and influence over the last seven days as I brought these words to life?

_____

_____

_____

_____

*Who, specifically, could benefit from these words? I sent this message to _____ (name(s)) on _____ (date).

WEEK **SIXTEEN**

The self-talk that you are playing is on an 8-track tape! You need an upgrade!

FRAMING QUESTIONS
Spark introspection, self-conversation, interpersonal conversation, and intentional action by answering these questions:

What do these words mean to me? How do they apply to my life?

_____

_____

_____

_____

What themes and takeaways do I have from reading this message?

_____

_____

_____

_____

What action will I take today/this week to apply and live these words?

_____

_____

_____

_____

What have I actually done in the past seven days to live these words?

_____

_____

_____

_____

What change have I seen in myself as a result of bringing these words to life over the last seven days?

_____

_____

_____

_____

How do I plan to be different now that I have meditated on and ingested these words?

_____

_____

_____

_____

Whose life did I impact and influence over the last seven days as I brought these words to life?

_____

_____

_____

_____

*Who, specifically, could benefit from these words? I sent this message to _____ (name(s)) on _____ (date).

WEEK **SEVENTEEN**

Friends and family...so many of you, at this very moment, are in the valley – trudging through the hard times and the dark days. Too many are divorcing; contemplating suicide; dying daily, in dead-end jobs, and working diligently to destroy yourselves through substance abuse, anger, and hatred. If I could just look into your eyes and soul right now, I'm telling you, YOU CAN MAKE IT! Your end is not here!

FRAMING QUESTIONS

Spark introspection, self-conversation, interpersonal conversation, and intentional action by answering these questions:

What do these words mean to me? How do they apply to my life?

_____

_____

_____

_____

What themes and takeaways do I have from reading this message?

_____

_____

_____

_____

What action will I take today/this week to apply and live these words?

_____

_____

_____

_____

What have I actually done in the past seven days to live these words?

_____

_____

_____

_____

What change have I seen in myself as a result of bringing these words to life over the last seven days?

_____

_____

_____

_____

How do I plan to be different now that I have meditated on and ingested these words?

_____

_____

_____

_____

Whose life did I impact and influence over the last seven days as I brought these words to life?

_____

_____

_____

_____

*Who, specifically, could benefit from these words? I sent this message to _____ (name(s)) on _____ (date).

WEEK **EIGHTEEN**

If you are looking for a sign...the sign is YOU...you have been given another day, another opportunity to make forward progress and either capture or reclaim what is yours. REFUSE to lose to the storm or adversity, for they are only temporary!

FRAMING QUESTIONS
Spark introspection, self-conversation, interpersonal conversation, and intentional action by answering these questions:

What do these words mean to me? How do they apply to my life?

_____

_____

_____

_____

What themes and takeaways do I have from reading this message?

_____

_____

_____

_____

What action will I take today/this week to apply and live these words?

_____

_____

_____

_____

What have I actually done in the past seven days to live these words?

_____

_____

_____

_____

What change have I seen in myself as a result of bringing these words to life over the last seven days?

_____

_____

_____

_____

How do I plan to be different now that I have meditated on and ingested these words?

_____

_____

_____

_____

Whose life did I impact and influence over the last seven days as I brought these words to life?

_____

_____

_____

_____

*Who, specifically, could benefit from these words? I sent this message to _____ (name(s)) on _____ (date).

WEEK **NINETEEN**

A person who feels hatred for, fosters harmful designs against, or engages in antagonistic activities against another - an adversary or opponent - THIS is an enemy! Let's stop placing people in this category that simply do not belong! For the true enemies, we ready ourselves for battle! For the difficult folks that you encounter, go have a courageous conversation and do all that you can to WORK through the challenges! There are no victims here to feed on! People, know that your ability to distinguish between enemy and "difficult to deal with" is the difference between life and death, living and dying, insanity and peace!

FRAMING QUESTIONS

Spark introspection, self-conversation, interpersonal conversation, and intentional action by answering these questions:

What do these words mean to me? How do they apply to my life?

_____

_____

_____

_____

What themes and takeaways do I have from reading this message?

_____

_____

_____

_____

What action will I take today/this week to apply and live these words?

_____

_____

_____

_____

What have I actually done in the past seven days to live these words?

_____

_____

_____

_____

What change have I seen in myself as a result of bringing these words to life over the last seven days?

_____

_____

_____

_____

How do I plan to be different now that I have meditated on and ingested these words?

_____

_____

_____

_____

Whose life did I impact and influence over the last seven days as I brought these words to life?

_____

_____

_____

_____

*Who, specifically, could benefit from these words? I sent this message to _____ (name(s)) on _____ (date).

WEEK **TWENTY**

If you are thinking about not forgiving someone, think about all of the times that you have been forgiven, escaped punishment for something you did, or you were able to side-step harm that was certainly coming your way. That same love, grace, and mercy you received – pay it forward!

FRAMING QUESTIONS

Spark introspection, self-conversation, interpersonal conversation, and intentional action by answering these questions:

What do these words mean to me? How do they apply to my life?

_____

_____

_____

_____

What themes and takeaways do I have from reading this message?

_____

_____

_____

_____

What action will I take today/this week to apply and live these words?

_____

_____

_____

_____

What have I actually done in the past seven days to live these words?

_____

_____

_____

_____

What change have I seen in myself as a result of bringing these words to life over the last seven days?

_____

_____

_____

_____

How do I plan to be different now that I have meditated on and ingested these words?

_____

_____

_____

_____

Whose life did I impact and influence over the last seven days as I brought these words to life?

_____

_____

_____

_____

*Who, specifically, could benefit from these words? I sent this message to _____ (name(s)) on _____ (date).

WEEK **TWENTY-ONE**

Finding peace and joy in the time spent with self is a treasure; and it is of greater value if you can take that peaceful and joyful self and invest it in others and the strengthening of relationships! Family, friends, and the perfect stranger deserve the best you that you can build!

FRAMING QUESTIONS

Spark introspection, self-conversation, interpersonal conversation, and intentional action by answering these questions:

What do these words mean to me? How do they apply to my life?

_____

_____

_____

_____

What themes and takeaways do I have from reading this message?

_____

_____

_____

_____

What action will I take today/this week to apply and live these words?

_____

_____

_____

_____

What have I actually done in the past seven days to live these words?

_____

_____

_____

_____

What change have I seen in myself as a result of bringing these words to life over the last seven days?

_____

_____

_____

_____

How do I plan to be different now that I have meditated on and ingested these words?

_____

_____

_____

_____

Whose life did I impact and influence over the last seven days as I brought these words to life?

_____

_____

_____

_____

*Who, specifically, could benefit from these words? I sent this message to _____ (name(s)) on _____ (date).

WEEK **TWENTY-TWO**

The first step to discovering that you can do anything is to dream, think about what could be, and imagine the possibilities! Free thy mind so "believing" can find you and make a home in your spirit, speak from your heart, and become one with your purpose!

FRAMING QUESTIONS

Spark introspection, self-conversation, interpersonal conversation, and intentional action by answering these questions:

What do these words mean to me? How do they apply to my life?

_____

_____

_____

_____

What themes and takeaways do I have from reading this message?

_____

_____

_____

_____

What action will I take today/this week to apply and live these words?

_____

_____

_____

_____

What have I actually done in the past seven days to live these words?

_____

_____

_____

_____

What change have I seen in myself as a result of bringing these words to life over the last seven days?

_____

_____

_____

How do I plan to be different now that I have meditated on and ingested these words?

_____

_____

_____

Whose life did I impact and influence over the last seven days as I brought these words to life?

_____

_____

_____

*Who, specifically, could benefit from these words? I sent this message to _____ (name(s)) on _____ (date).

WEEK TWENTY-THREE

Not if, but when you have the opportunity to be in the presence of greatness, SIT DOWN; touch it to learn how it feels; observe it to see how it moves and maneuvers; taste it to get it inside your spirit; smell it to know that it is right and understand what legacy it leaves behind; and listen to gain its wisdom. And, your mission is to duplicate and exceed the level of greatness that you can now sense!

FRAMING QUESTIONS

Spark introspection, self-conversation, interpersonal conversation, and intentional action by answering these questions:

What do these words mean to me? How do they apply to my life?

_____

_____

_____

_____

What themes and takeaways do I have from reading this message?

_____

_____

_____

_____

What action will I take today/this week to apply and live these words?

_____

_____

_____

_____

What have I actually done in the past seven days to live these words?

_____

_____

_____

_____

What change have I seen in myself as a result of bringing these words to life over the last seven days?

_____

_____

_____

_____

How do I plan to be different now that I have meditated on and ingested these words?

_____

_____

_____

_____

Whose life did I impact and influence over the last seven days as I brought these words to life?

_____

_____

_____

_____

*Who, specifically, could benefit from these words? I sent this message to _____ (name(s)) on _____ (date).

WEEK **TWENTY-FOUR**

The advice of any ordinary, everyday person is just as great as any of our historical, famous, and infamous figures...once questioned and tested!

FRAMING QUESTIONS

Spark introspection, self-conversation, interpersonal conversation, and intentional action by answering these questions:

What Do These Words Mean To Me? How Do They Apply To My Life?

_____

_____

_____

_____

What Themes And Takeaways Do I Have From Reading This Message?

_____

_____

_____

_____

What Action Will I Take Today/This Week To Apply And Live These Words?

_____

_____

_____

_____

What Did I Actually Do The Past Seven Days To Live These Words?

_____

_____

_____

_____

What Change Did I See In Myself As A Result Of Bringing These Words To Life Over The Last Seven Days?

_____

_____

_____

_____

How Do I Plan To Be Different Now That I Have Meditated On And Ingested These Words?

_____

_____

_____

_____

Whose Life Did I Impact And Influence Over The Last Seven Days As I Brought These Words To Life?

_____

_____

_____

_____

*Who, specifically, could benefit from these words? I sent this message to _____ (name(s)) on _____ (date).

WEEK TWENTY-FIVE

Work diligently to fix the relationships with even your perceived enemies and you'll find a greater ease to living and a livelier beat in your heart! Unnecessary discord distances us from life!

FRAMING QUESTIONS

Spark introspection, self-conversation, interpersonal conversation, and intentional action by answering these questions:

What do these words mean to me? How do they apply to my life?

_____

_____

_____

_____

What themes and takeaways do I have from reading this message?

_____

_____

_____

_____

What action will I take today/this week to apply and live these words?

_____

_____

_____

_____

What have I actually done in the past seven days to live these words?

_____

_____

_____

_____

What change have I seen in myself as a result of bringing these words to life over the last seven days?

_____

_____

_____

_____

How do I plan to be different now that I have meditated on and ingested these words?

_____

_____

_____

_____

Whose life did I impact and influence over the last seven days as I brought these words to life?

_____

_____

_____

_____

*Who, specifically, could benefit from these words? I sent this message to _____ (name(s)) on _____ (date).

WEEK **TWENTY-SIX**

Stop placing much of your energy into chasing and trying to identify the people who are trying to wrong you; instead, invest your search and discovery in your up-lifters, encouragers, and those with the mission to inspire you! You can either feed your hurt or your health!

FRAMING QUESTIONS
Spark introspection, self-conversation, interpersonal conversation, and intentional action by answering these questions:

What do these words mean to me? How do they apply to my life?

_____

_____

_____

_____

What themes and takeaways do I have from reading this message?

_____

_____

_____

_____

What action will I take today/this week to apply and live these words?

_____

_____

_____

_____

What have I actually done in the past seven days to live these words?

_____

_____

_____

_____

What change have I seen in myself as a result of bringing these words to life over the last seven days?

_____

_____

_____

_____

How do I plan to be different now that I have meditated on and ingested these words?

_____

_____

_____

_____

Whose life did I impact and influence over the last seven days as I brought these words to life?

_____

_____

_____

_____

*Who, specifically, could benefit from these words? I sent this message to _____ (name(s)) on _____ (date).

WEEK **TWENTY-SEVEN**

Carrying grudges is heavy weight that breaks backs and blocks blessings! Workout daily with forgiveness; it is much lighter and better for the heart!

FRAMING QUESTIONS
Spark introspection, self-conversation, interpersonal conversation, and intentional action by answering these questions:

What do these words mean to me? How do they apply to my life?

_____

_____

_____

_____

What themes and takeaways do I have from reading this message?

_____

_____

_____

_____

What action will I take today/this week to apply and live these words?

_____

_____

_____

_____

What have I actually done in the past seven days to live these words?

_____

_____

_____

_____

What change have I seen in myself as a result of bringing these words to life over the last seven days?

_____

_____

_____

_____

How do I plan to be different now that I have meditated on and ingested these words?

_____

_____

_____

_____

Whose life did I impact and influence over the last seven days as I brought these words to life?

_____

_____

_____

_____

*Who, specifically, could benefit from these words? I sent this message to _____ (name(s)) on _____ (date).

MID-YEAR REFLECTION

On a particular Monday, I was at Starbucks in the typical long, but fast-moving line. When I reached the waiting area where all of the "bucks" addicts wait for our chosen poison (in my case, iced vanilla green tea latte grande....itchy-gitchy-ya-ya-da-da (I digress). A well-dressed gentleman with a foreign accent said, "You look like the happiest person in that line. Wow! I mean...wow!" He said, "so many people just look so blah" (he even did the blah face and body motion, too). I said, "Thank you, Sir!"

Lesson learned and wisdom gained: No matter what I am going through or what baggage I am carrying, my joy cannot be stolen! When you think things are casual, someone is looking for a sign that things are better and that there is hope in the next person... enough to give themselves some hope! We are responsible for giving one another hope! And someone else noticing light in me enables me to see light at the end of the tunnel as well as in my immediate circumstances! Don't lose hope, people! Be excellent... even when things are not!

How has your journal journey been thus far?

Do you do things differently? If so, how? If not, why?

What is the goal for the next part of your journal journey?

Purposeful Action:

Think of a life instance wherein you learned a tremendous lesson and gain significant wisdom that changed your life and the way you journeyed through life from then on!

summer

Heal Thyself

Greatness is taking root and growing within you – and you want it to stay. So, you commit to healing so that the seeds of wisdom can take hold in the softer and readily available soil you have created. To want and need to heal is a conscious decision that you must continue to make until the scars you have accumulated have either faded or virtually disappeared. Time for you to be restored!

WEEK **TWENTY-EIGHT**

As long as what happens TO ME does not get IN ME, I cannot be defeated! Too often, situations and people get under our skin and begin to wreak havoc with our emotions and feelings. But, just as you decide what food enters your system, you CAN take an active role in how you respond to the uncertainty that life will certainly bring! The quality of my life and daily existence is up to me – not you!

FRAMING QUESTIONS
Spark introspection, self-conversation, interpersonal conversation, and intentional action by answering these questions:

What do these words mean to me? How do they apply to my life?

_____

_____

_____

_____

What themes and takeaways do I have from reading this message?

_____

_____

_____

_____

What action will I take today/this week to apply and live these words?

_____

_____

_____

_____

What have I actually done in the past seven days to live these words?

_____

_____

_____

_____

What change have I seen in myself as a result of bringing these words to life over the last seven days?

_____

_____

_____

_____

How do I plan to be different now that I have meditated on and ingested these words?

_____

_____

_____

_____

Whose life did I impact and influence over the last seven days as I brought these words to life?

_____

_____

_____

_____

*Who, specifically, could benefit from these words? I sent this message to _____ (name(s)) on _____ (date).

WEEK **TWENTY-NINE**

I know it seems like it...but you have not been forgotten! What you need is on the way! Have faith!

FRAMING QUESTIONS
Spark introspection, self-conversation, interpersonal conversation, and intentional action by answering these questions:

What do these words mean to me? How do they apply to my life?

_____

_____

_____

_____

What themes and takeaways do I have from reading this message?

_____

_____

_____

_____

What action will I take today/this week to apply and live these words?

_____

_____

_____

_____

What have I actually done in the past seven days to live these words?

_____

_____

_____

_____

What change have I seen in myself as a result of bringing these words to life over the last seven days?

_____

_____

_____

How do I plan to be different now that I have meditated on and ingested these words?

_____

_____

_____

_____

Whose life did I impact and influence over the last seven days as I brought these words to life?

_____

_____

_____

_____

*Who, specifically, could benefit from these words? I sent this message to _____ (name(s)) on _____ (date).

WEEK **THIRTY**

I am vowing not to be anxious. For I trust the gift and potential in me, my lessons learned, and my spirit and faith that continue to grow and give courage! Everything working together has proven to me that, come what may, I will be okay!

FRAMING QUESTIONS
Spark introspection, self-conversation, interpersonal conversation, and intentional action by answering these questions:

What do these words mean to me? How do they apply to my life?

_____

_____

_____

_____

What themes and takeaways do I have from reading this message?

_____

_____

_____

_____

What action will I take today/this week to apply and live these words?

_____

_____

_____

_____

What have I actually done in the past seven days to live these words?

_____

_____

_____

_____

What change have I seen in myself as a result of bringing these words to life over the last seven days?

_____

_____

_____

_____

How do I plan to be different now that I have meditated on and ingested these words?

_____

_____

_____

_____

Whose life did I impact and influence over the last seven days as I brought these words to life?

_____

_____

_____

_____

*Who, specifically, could benefit from these words? I sent this message to _____ (name(s)) on _____ (date).

WEEK **THIRTY-ONE**

'Tis an odd place - some may call it hell - to be in when you have a deep need and yet you do not want to be a bother to anyone! Herein lies your life choice; Do you need help or will you continue not to be a bother?

FRAMING QUESTIONS
Spark introspection, self-conversation, interpersonal conversation, and intentional action by answering these questions:

What do these words mean to me? How do they apply to my life?

_____

_____

_____

_____

What themes and takeaways do I have from reading this message?

_____

_____

_____

_____

What action will I take today/this week to apply and live these words?

_____

_____

_____

_____

What have I actually done in the past seven days to live these words?

_____

_____

_____

_____

What change have I seen in myself as a result of bringing these words to life over the last seven days?

_____

_____

_____

How do I plan to be different now that I have meditated on and ingested these words?

_____

_____

_____

_____

Whose life did I impact and influence over the last seven days as I brought these words to life?

_____

_____

_____

_____

*Who, specifically, could benefit from these words? I sent this message to _____ (name(s)) on _____ (date).

WEEK **THIRTY-TWO**

I know...your heart and spirit were hurt while being vulnerable. But, like having to go BEHIND the wall to repair a leak, how beautifully ironic is it that you must return to vulnerability for repair, healing, and restoration to take place? Do not be afraid...there is indeed strength in vulnerability!

FRAMING QUESTIONS
Spark introspection, self-conversation, interpersonal conversation, and intentional action by answering these questions:

What do these words mean to me? How do they apply to my life?

_____

_____

_____

_____

What themes and takeaways do I have from reading this message?

_____

_____

_____

_____

What action will I take today/this week to apply and live these words?

_____

_____

_____

_____

What have I actually done in the past seven days to live these words?

_____

_____

_____

_____

What change have I seen in myself as a result of bringing these words to life over the last seven days?

_____

_____

_____

_____

How do I plan to be different now that I have meditated on and ingested these words?

_____

_____

_____

_____

Whose life did I impact and influence over the last seven days as I brought these words to life?

_____

_____

_____

_____

*Who, specifically, could benefit from these words? I sent this message to _____ (name(s)) on _____ (date).

WEEK **THIRTY-THREE**

Simply because someone is lost does not mean that they cannot give you directions to where you are going! LISTEN FOR THE WISDOM IN ALL THINGS!

FRAMING QUESTIONS
Spark introspection, self-conversation, interpersonal conversation, and intentional action by answering these questions:

What do these words mean to me? How do they apply to my life?

_____

_____

_____

_____

What themes and takeaways do I have from reading this message?

_____

_____

_____

_____

What action will I take today/this week to apply and live these words?

_____

_____

_____

_____

What have I actually done in the past seven days to live these words?

_____

_____

_____

_____

What change have I seen in myself as a result of bringing these words to life over the last seven days?

_____

_____

_____

_____

How do I plan to be different now that I have meditated on and ingested these words?

_____

_____

_____

_____

Whose life did I impact and influence over the last seven days as I brought these words to life?

_____

_____

_____

_____

*Who, specifically, could benefit from these words? I sent this message to _____ (name(s)) on _____ (date).

WEEK **THIRTY-FOUR**

If you promote your pain and struggle, make resentment your focus, and hide your vulnerability, then you make way for the wrong people to enter your life – folks who aim to co-sign your pain, as opposed to helping lift your burdens and extinguish your anxiety. We NEED people who force us to dream and motivate us to action. Let us be mindful of the energy and spirit we maintain and be ever careful of the company that we keep!

FRAMING QUESTIONS

Spark introspection, self-conversation, interpersonal conversation, and intentional action by answering these questions:

What do these words mean to me? How do they apply to my life?

_____

_____

_____

_____

What themes and takeaways do I have from reading this message?

_____

_____

_____

_____

What action will I take today/this week to apply and live these words?

_____

_____

_____

_____

What have I actually done in the past seven days to live these words?

_____

_____

_____

_____

What change have I seen in myself as a result of bringing these words to life over the last seven days?

_____

_____

_____

How do I plan to be different now that I have meditated on and ingested these words?

_____

_____

_____

_____

Whose life did I impact and influence over the last seven days as I brought these words to life?

_____

_____

_____

_____

*Who, specifically, could benefit from these words? I sent this message to _____ (name(s)) on _____ (date).

WEEK **THIRTY-FIVE**

You think that the problem stands in front of you? No! The problem stands inside of you and you have not yet willed it to move back and move on so that all of you can come forth!

FRAMING QUESTIONS
Spark introspection, self-conversation, interpersonal conversation, and intentional action by answering these questions:

What do these words mean to me? How do they apply to my life?

_____

_____

_____

_____

What themes and takeaways do I have from reading this message?

_____

_____

_____

_____

What action will I take today/this week to apply and live these words?

_____

_____

_____

_____

What have I actually done in the past seven days to live these words?

_____

_____

_____

_____

What change have I seen in myself as a result of bringing these words to life over the last seven days?

_____

_____

_____

_____

How do I plan to be different now that I have meditated on and ingested these words?

_____

_____

_____

_____

Whose life did I impact and influence over the last seven days as I brought these words to life?

_____

_____

_____

_____

*Who, specifically, could benefit from these words? I sent this message to _____ (name(s)) on _____ (date).

WEEK **THIRTY-SIX**

Surrender to your own greatness within, taking every dare to do what it is you are destined to do. Live in purpose, with purpose, on purpose!

FRAMING QUESTIONS
Spark introspection, self-conversation, interpersonal conversation, and intentional action by answering these questions:

What do these words mean to me? How do they apply to my life?

_____

_____

_____

_____

What themes and takeaways do I have from reading this message?

_____

_____

_____

_____

What action will I take today/this week to apply and live these words?

_____

_____

_____

_____

What have I actually done in the past seven days to live these words?

_____

_____

_____

_____

What change have I seen in myself as a result of bringing these words to life over the last seven days?

_____

_____

_____

_____

How do I plan to be different now that I have meditated on and ingested these words?

_____

_____

_____

_____

Whose life did I impact and influence over the last seven days as I brought these words to life?

_____

_____

_____

_____

*Who, specifically, could benefit from these words? I sent this message to _____ (name(s)) on _____ (date).

WEEK **THIRTY-SEVEN**

When you get over the obstacle of yourself, you will find a line of people on the other side who have been waiting for your arrival, your gifts, and your purpose!

FRAMING QUESTIONS
Spark introspection, self-conversation, interpersonal conversation, and intentional action by answering these questions:

What do these words mean to me? How do they apply to my life?

_____

_____

_____

_____

What themes and takeaways do I have from reading this message?

_____

_____

_____

_____

What action will I take today/this week to apply and live these words?

_____

_____

_____

_____

What have I actually done in the past seven days to live these words?

_____

_____

_____

_____

What change have I seen in myself as a result of bringing these words to life over the last seven days?

_____

_____

_____

_____

How do I plan to be different now that I have meditated on and ingested these words?

_____

_____

_____

_____

Whose life did I impact and influence over the last seven days as I brought these words to life?

_____

_____

_____

_____

*Who, specifically, could benefit from these words? I sent this message to _____ (name(s)) on _____ (date).

WEEK **THIRTY-EIGHT**

Be great, be encouraged, be purposeful, be gifted, and be of service...for the life you save may be your very own!

FRAMING QUESTIONS
Spark introspection, self-conversation, interpersonal conversation, and intentional action by answering these questions:

What do these words mean to me? How do they apply to my life?

_____

_____

_____

_____

What themes and takeaways do I have from reading this message?

_____

_____

_____

_____

What action will I take today/this week to apply and live these words?

_____

_____

_____

_____

What have I actually done in the past seven days to live these words?

_____

_____

_____

_____

What change have I seen in myself as a result of bringing these words to life over the last seven days?

_____

_____

_____

_____

How do I plan to be different now that I have meditated on and ingested these words?

_____

_____

_____

_____

Whose life did I impact and influence over the last seven days as I brought these words to life?

_____

_____

_____

_____

*Who, specifically, could benefit from these words? I sent this message to _____ (name(s)) on _____ (date).

WEEK **THIRTY-NINE**

YES, change may be a leap toward excellence and even the order for the moment but, the manner in which you change – willfully and with grace and honor – is monumental!

FRAMING QUESTIONS
Spark introspection, self-conversation, interpersonal conversation, and intentional action by answering these questions:

What do these words mean to me? How do they apply to my life?

_____

_____

_____

_____

What themes and takeaways do I have from reading this message?

_____

_____

_____

_____

What action will I take today/this week to apply and live these words?

_____

_____

_____

_____

What have I actually done in the past seven days to live these words?

_____

_____

_____

_____

What change have I seen in myself as a result of bringing these words to life over the last seven days?

_____

_____

_____

_____

How do I plan to be different now that I have meditated on and ingested these words?

_____

_____

_____

_____

Whose life did I impact and influence over the last seven days as I brought these words to life?

_____

_____

_____

_____

*Who, specifically, could benefit from these words? I sent this message to _____ (name(s)) on _____ (date).

WEEK **FORTY**

Every enemy that presents himself as such, is not. And each friend that claims to be, is not. Therefore, keep discernment close! For it sees through to the true heart of the professed enemies and friends!

FRAMING QUESTIONS
Spark introspection, self-conversation, interpersonal conversation, and intentional action by answering these questions:

What do these words mean to me? How do they apply to my life?

_____

_____

_____

_____

What themes and takeaways do I have from reading this message?

_____

_____

_____

_____

What action will I take today/this week to apply and live these words?

_____

_____

_____

_____

What have I actually done in the past seven days to live these words?

_____

_____

_____

_____

What change have I seen in myself as a result of bringing these words to life over the last seven days?

_____

_____

_____

_____

How do I plan to be different now that I have meditated on and ingested these words?

_____

_____

_____

_____

Whose life did I impact and influence over the last seven days as I brought these words to life?

_____

_____

_____

_____

*Who, specifically, could benefit from these words? I sent this message to _____ (name(s)) on _____ (date).

fall

Fear-less-ness

Courage is growing within you daily. You feel your limbs getting stronger and growing, toward the sun. Your spirit is healing and beginning to shine. You are moving toward being a worthy opponent against the fear that you encounter. You will win! And you are going to be able to withstand the winds and any storm...joyfully.

WEEK **FORTY-ONE**

FEAR! Today, you cannot have anything...my family, me, my friends, my opportunity, my next steps, my day, my journey, my past, my present, nor anything that is to come! And, you certainly cannot have my purpose! FEAR! The ONLY way for you to get my time is if it is spent conquering you!

FRAMING QUESTIONS
Spark introspection, self-conversation, interpersonal conversation, and intentional action by answering these questions:

What do these words mean to me? How do they apply to my life?

_____

_____

_____

_____

What themes and takeaways do I have from reading this message?

_____

_____

_____

_____

What action will I take today/this week to apply and live these words?

_____

_____

_____

_____

What have I actually done in the past seven days to live these words?

_____

_____

_____

_____

What change have I seen in myself as a result of bringing these words to life over the last seven days?

_____

_____

_____

_____

How do I plan to be different now that I have meditated on and ingested these words?

_____

_____

_____

_____

Whose life did I impact and influence over the last seven days as I brought these words to life?

_____

_____

_____

_____

*Who, specifically, could benefit from these words? I sent this message to _____ (name(s)) on _____ (date).

WEEK **FORTY-TWO**

Fear...I see you! The more tactics you try, the more you think you will make me quake at the sound of your name. But, with every encounter, I know you more and replace you with courage. Soon, you will pass me by because you will see less of you in me. You will then be a victim of my success.

FRAMING QUESTIONS
Spark introspection, self-conversation, interpersonal conversation, and intentional action by answering these questions:

What do these words mean to me? How do they apply to my life?

_____

_____

_____

_____

What themes and takeaways do I have from reading this message?

_____

_____

_____

_____

What action will I take today/this week to apply and live these words?

_____

_____

_____

_____

What have I actually done in the past seven days to live these words?

_____

_____

_____

_____

What change have I seen in myself as a result of bringing these words to life over the last seven days?

_____

_____

_____

_____

How do I plan to be different now that I have meditated on and ingested these words?

_____

_____

_____

_____

Whose life did I impact and influence over the last seven days as I brought these words to life?

_____

_____

_____

_____

*Who, specifically, could benefit from these words? I sent this message to _____ (name(s)) on _____ (date).

WEEK **FORTY-THREE**

You shall live and not die!!! A powerful verse to help you combat physical conditions, but what if you took this verse into every situation that you thought was dead or destroyed? Imagine how victorious you would be! We shall live and NOT die!

FRAMING QUESTIONS
Spark introspection, self-conversation, interpersonal conversation, and intentional action by answering these questions:

What do these words mean to me? How do they apply to my life?

_____

_____

_____

_____

What themes and takeaways do I have from reading this message?

_____

_____

_____

_____

What action will I take today/this week to apply and live these words?

_____

_____

_____

_____

What have I actually done in the past seven days to live these words?

_____

_____

_____

_____

What change have I seen in myself as a result of bringing these words to life over the last seven days?

_____

_____

_____

How do I plan to be different now that I have meditated on and ingested these words?

_____

_____

_____

_____

Whose life did I impact and influence over the last seven days as I brought these words to life?

_____

_____

_____

*Who, specifically, could benefit from these words? I sent this message to _____ (name(s)) on _____ (date).

WEEK **FORTY-FOUR**

Remember, the unprepared is one of fear's favorite meals! Your job, should you choose to accept it, is to starve fear!

FRAMING QUESTIONS

Spark introspection, self-conversation, interpersonal conversation, and intentional action by answering these questions:

What do these words mean to me? How do they apply to my life?

_____

_____

_____

_____

What themes and takeaways do I have from reading this message?

_____

_____

_____

_____

What action will I take today/this week to apply and live these words?

_____

_____

_____

_____

What have I actually done in the past seven days to live these words?

_____

_____

_____

_____

What change have I seen in myself as a result of bringing these words to life over the last seven days?

_____

_____

_____

_____

How do I plan to be different now that I have meditated on and ingested these words?

_____

_____

_____

_____

Whose life did I impact and influence over the last seven days as I brought these words to life?

_____

_____

_____

_____

*Who, specifically, could benefit from these words? I sent this message to _____ (name(s)) on _____ (date).

WEEK **FORTY-FIVE**

Fear! It will torture you as long as you continually look away from it! But, once you fully turn toward it, face it, give it your undivided stare, and unceasingly and deliberately move in its direction, fear will flee!

FRAMING QUESTIONS
Spark introspection, self-conversation, interpersonal conversation, and intentional action by answering these questions:

What do these words mean to me? How do they apply to my life?

_____

_____

_____

_____

What themes and takeaways do I have from reading this message?

_____

_____

_____

_____

What action will I take today/this week to apply and live these words?

_____

_____

_____

_____

What have I actually done in the past seven days to live these words?

_____

_____

_____

_____

What change have I seen in myself as a result of bringing these words to life over the last seven days?

_____

_____

_____

_____

How do I plan to be different now that I have meditated on and ingested these words?

_____

_____

_____

_____

Whose life did I impact and influence over the last seven days as I brought these words to life?

_____

_____

_____

_____

*Who, specifically, could benefit from these words? I sent this message to _____ (name(s)) on _____ (date).

WEEK **FORTY-SIX**

Before we die, each day that we are graced with should be filled with effort, purpose, energy, and willpower to heal from what has kept us from living!

FRAMING QUESTIONS
Spark introspection, self-conversation, interpersonal conversation, and intentional action by answering these questions:

What do these words mean to me? How do they apply to my life?

_____

_____

_____

_____

What themes and takeaways do I have from reading this message?

_____

_____

_____

_____

What action will I take today/this week to apply and live these words?

_____

_____

_____

_____

What have I actually done in the past seven days to live these words?

_____

_____

_____

_____

What change have I seen in myself as a result of bringing these words to life over the last seven days?

_____

_____

_____

_____

How do I plan to be different now that I have meditated on and ingested these words?

_____

_____

_____

_____

Whose life did I impact and influence over the last seven days as I brought these words to life?

_____

_____

_____

_____

*Who, specifically, could benefit from these words? I sent this message to _____ (name(s)) on _____ (date).

WEEK **FORTY-SEVEN**

Fear is a daily fight...and one in which I pray daily to be given yet another sunrise so as to continue my battle! And, through this journey – with each sunset reached and opportunity given – I become more fearless!

FRAMING QUESTIONS
Spark introspection, self-conversation, interpersonal conversation, and intentional action by answering these questions:

What do these words mean to me? How do they apply to my life?

_____

_____

_____

_____

What themes and takeaways do I have from reading this message?

_____

_____

_____

_____

What action will I take today/this week to apply and live these words?

_____

_____

_____

_____

What have I actually done in the past seven days to live these words?

_____

_____

_____

_____

What change have I seen in myself as a result of bringing these words to life over the last seven days?

_____

_____

_____

_____

How do I plan to be different now that I have meditated on and ingested these words?

_____

_____

_____

_____

Whose life did I impact and influence over the last seven days as I brought these words to life?

_____

_____

_____

_____

*Who, specifically, could benefit from these words? I sent this message to _____ **(name(s)) on** _____ **(date).**

WEEK **FORTY-EIGHT**

Trust in your gift, for it guards you against people who don't trust in it. You should not believe that you have no purpose.

FRAMING QUESTIONS
Spark introspection, self-conversation, interpersonal conversation, and intentional action by answering these questions:

What do these words mean to me? How do they apply to my life?

_____

_____

_____

_____

What themes and takeaways do I have from reading this message?

_____

_____

_____

_____

What action will I take today/this week to apply and live these words?

_____

_____

_____

_____

What have I actually done in the past seven days to live these words?

_____

_____

_____

_____

What change have I seen in myself as a result of bringing these words to life over the last seven days?

_____

_____

_____

_____

How do I plan to be different now that I have meditated on and ingested these words?

_____

_____

_____

_____

Whose life did I impact and influence over the last seven days as I brought these words to life?

_____

_____

_____

_____

*Who, specifically, could benefit from these words? I sent this message to _____ (name(s)) on _____ (date).

WEEK **FORTY-NINE**

I am betting that you can...unless you are betting you cannot! For some, YOUR logic has gotten the best of you, and you have lost the ability to think outside of what you think could happen! And, this is often the difference between cannot and can!

FRAMING QUESTIONS
Spark introspection, self-conversation, interpersonal conversation, and intentional action by answering these questions:

What do these words mean to me? How do they apply to my life?

_____

_____

_____

_____

What themes and takeaways do I have from reading this message?

_____

_____

_____

_____

What action will I take today/this week to apply and live these words?

_____

_____

_____

_____

What have I actually done in the past seven days to live these words?

_____

_____

_____

_____

What change have I seen in myself as a result of bringing these words to life over the last seven days?

_____

_____

_____

_____

How do I plan to be different now that I have meditated on and ingested these words?

_____

_____

_____

_____

Whose life did I impact and influence over the last seven days as I brought these words to life?

_____

_____

_____

_____

*Who, specifically, could benefit from these words? I sent this message to _____ (name(s)) on _____ (date).

WEEK **FIFTY**

If there are some issues that you would not want to die having not resolved, then you should not want to live another day having not addressed those very same issues! The time is now!

FRAMING QUESTIONS
Spark introspection, self-conversation, interpersonal conversation, and intentional action by answering these questions:

What do these words mean to me? How do they apply to my life?

_____

_____

_____

_____

What themes and takeaways do I have from reading this message?

_____

_____

_____

_____

What action will I take today/this week to apply and live these words?

_____

_____

_____

_____

What have I actually done in the past seven days to live these words?

_____

_____

_____

_____

What change have I seen in myself as a result of bringing these words to life over the last seven days?

_____

_____

_____

_____

How do I plan to be different now that I have meditated on and ingested these words?

_____

_____

_____

_____

Whose life did I impact and influence over the last seven days as I brought these words to life?

_____

_____

_____

_____

*Who, specifically, could benefit from these words? I sent this message to _____ (name(s)) on _____ (date).

WEEK **FIFTY-ONE**

A sign that you are going to be okay is you coming to grips with the fact that you are currently not okay! It is your ability to hear and receive the hard messages and then make an unbreakable agreement with yourself that you are going toward WORK to be okay!

<u>FRAMING QUESTIONS</u>
Spark introspection, self-conversation, interpersonal conversation, and intentional action by answering these questions:

What do these words mean to me? How do they apply to my life?

_____

_____

_____

_____

What themes and takeaways do I have from reading this message?

_____

_____

_____

_____

What action will I take today/this week to apply and live these words?

_____

_____

_____

_____

What have I actually done in the past seven days to live these words?

_____

_____

_____

_____

What change have I seen in myself as a result of bringing these words to life over the last seven days?

_____

_____

_____

_____

How do I plan to be different now that I have meditated on and ingested these words?

_____

_____

_____

_____

Whose life did I impact and influence over the last seven days as I brought these words to life?

_____

_____

_____

_____

*Who, specifically, could benefit from these words? I sent this message to _____ (name(s)) on _____ (date).

WEEK **FIFTY-TWO**

My gift is greater than my fear!

FRAMING QUESTIONS
Spark introspection, self-conversation, interpersonal conversation, and intentional action by answering these questions:

What do these words mean to me? How do they apply to my life?

_____

_____

_____

_____

What themes and takeaways do I have from reading this message?

_____

_____

_____

_____

What action will I take today/this week to apply and live these words?

_____

_____

_____

_____

What have I actually done in the past seven days to live these words?

_____

_____

_____

_____

What change have I seen in myself as a result of bringing these words to life over the last seven days?

_____

_____

_____

_____

How do I plan to be different now that I have meditated on and ingested these words?

_____

_____

_____

_____

Whose life did I impact and influence over the last seven days as I brought these words to life?

_____

_____

_____

_____

*Who, specifically, could benefit from these words? I sent this message to
_____ (name(s)) on _____ (date).

NOW THAT YOU HAVE JOURNEYED

Celebrate yourself as well as your consistency and bravery shown by holding up the mirror to yourself and committing to your development for the better. I am hopeful that when the opportunities come and the people - some awaiting your rise, others awaiting your fall, and still others expecting nothing at all - are before you, that your legs do not tire and you have enough strength to defend the gift in you by humbly freeing and displaying its power!

What were your lessons learned during your journey?

_____

_____

Have you changed? And, how have you changed?

_____

_____

Did you help others along the way?

_____

_____

What was your greatest wisdom gained during your journey?

_____

_____

Made in the USA
Lexington, KY
22 April 2015